KAREN
BLIXEN
(ISAK DINESEN)

FROM THE NGONG HILLS

D1348385

PENGUIN BOOKS

PENGUIN BOOKS

Published by the Penguin Group. Penguin Books Ltd, 27 Wrights Lane, London
w8 5tz, England. Penguin Books USA Inc., 375 Hudson Street, New York,
New York 10014, USA. Penguin Books Australia Ltd, Ringwood, Victoria, Australia.
Penguin Books Canada Ltd, 10 Alcorn Avenue, Toronto, Ontario, Canada m4v 3b2.
Penguin Books (NZ) Ltd, 182–190 Wairau Road, Auckland 10, New Zealand · Penguin
Books Ltd, Registered Offices: Harmondsworth, Middlesex, England · These extracts
are from *Out of Africa*, by Karen Blixen (Isak Dinesen), published in Penguin Books
1954. This edition published 1996. Copyright © 1937 by Karen Blixen. All rights
reserved · Typeset by Rowland Phototypesetting Ltd, Bury St Edmunds, Suffolk.
Printed in England by Clays Ltd, St Ives plc · Except in the United States of America,
this book is sold subject to the condition that it shall not, by way of trade or otherwise,
be lent, re-sold, hired out, or otherwise circulated without the publisher's prior
consent in any form of binding or cover other than that in which it is published and
without a similar condition including this condition being imposed on the subsequent
purchaser · 10 9 8 7 6 5 4 3 2 1

From the forests and highlands
We come, we come.

CONTENTS

The Ngong Farm

I had a farm in Africa, at the foot of the Ngong Hills. The Equator runs across these highlands, a hundred miles to the north, and the farm lay at an altitude of over six thousand feet. In the day-time you felt that you had got high up, near to the sun, but the early mornings and evenings were limpid and restful, and the nights were cold.

The geographical position and the height of the land combined to create a landscape that had not its like in all the world. There was no fat on it and no luxuriance anywhere; it was Africa distilled up through six thousand feet, like the strong and refined essence of a continent. The colours were dry and burnt, like the colours in pottery. The trees had a light delicate foliage, the structure of which was different from that of the trees in Europe; it did not grow in bows or cupolas, but in horizontal layers, and the formation gave to the tall solitary trees a likeness to the palms, or a heroic and romantic air like full-rigged ships with their sails furled, and to the edge of a wood a strange appearance as if the whole wood were faintly vibrating. Upon the grass of the great plains the crooked bare old thorn-trees were scattered, and the grass was spiced like thyme and bog-myrtles; in some places the scent was so strong that it smarted in the nostrils. All the flowers that you found on the plains, or upon the creepers and liana in the native forest, were diminutive like flowers of the downs – only just in the beginning of the long rains a number of big, massive heavy-scented lilies sprang out on the plains. The views were immensely wide. Everything that you saw made for greatness and freedom, and unequalled nobility.

The chief feature of the landscape, and of your life in it, was the air. Looking back on a sojourn in the African highlands, you are struck by your feeling of having lived for a time up in the air. The sky was rarely more than pale blue or violet, with a profusion of mighty, weightless, ever-changing clouds towering up and sailing on it, but it had a blue vigour in it, and at a short distance it painted the ranges of hills and the woods a fresh deep blue. In the middle of the day the air was alive over the land, like a flame burning; it scintillated, waved and shone like running water, mirrored and doubled all objects, and created great Fata Morgana. Up in this high air you breathed easily, drawing in a vital assurance and lightness of heart. In the highlands you woke up in the morning and thought: Here I am, where I ought to be.

The Mountain of Ngong stretches in a long ridge from north to south, and is crowned with four noble peaks like immovable darker blue waves against the sky. It rises eight thousand feet above the sea, and to the east two thousand feet above the surrounding country; but to the west the drop is deeper and more precipitous – the hills fall vertically down towards the Great Rift Valley.

The wind in the highlands blows steadily from the north–north-east. It is the same wind that, down at the coasts of Africa and Arabia, they name the Monsoon, the East Wind, which was King Solomon's favourite horse. Up here it is felt as just the resistance of the air, as the earth throws herself forward into space. The wind runs straight against the Ngong Hills, and the slopes of the hills would be the ideal place for setting up a glider, that would be lifted upwards by the currents, over the mountain top. The clouds, which were travelling with the wind, struck the side of the hill and hung round it, or were caught on the summit and broke into rain. But those that took a higher course and sailed clear of the reef, dissolved to the west of it, over the burning desert of the Rift Valley. Many times I have from my house followed these mighty processions advancing, and have wondered to see their proud floating masses, as soon as they had got over the hills, vanish in the blue air and be gone.

The hills from the farm changed their character many times in the course of the day, and sometimes looked quite close, and at other times very far away. In the evening, when it was getting dark, it would first look, as you gazed at them, as if in the sky a thin silver line was drawn all along the silhouette of the dark mountain; then, as night fell, the four peaks seemed to be flattened and smoothened out, as if the mountain was stretching and spreading itself.

From the Ngong Hills you have a unique view, you see to the south the vast plains of the great game-country that stretches all the way to Kilimanjaro; to the east and north the park-like country of the foot-hills with the forest behind them, and the undulating land of the Kikuyu Reserve, which extends to Mount Kenya a hundred miles away – a mosaic of little square maize-fields, banana-groves and grassland, with here and there the blue smoke from a native village, a small cluster of peaked mole-casts. But towards the west,

4

deep down, lies the dry, moon-like landscape of the African low country. The brown desert is irregularly dotted with the little marks of the thornbushes, the winding river-beds are drawn up with crooked dark-green trails; those are the woods of the mighty, wide-branching mimosa trees, with thorns like spikes; the cactus grows here, and here is the home of the giraffe and the rhino.

The hill-country itself, when you get into it, is tremendously big, picturesque and mysterious; varied with long valleys, thickets, green slopes, and rocky crags. High up, under one of the peaks, there is even a bamboo-grove. There are springs and wells in the hills; I have camped up here by them.

In my day, the buffalo, the eland and the rhino lived in the Ngong Hills; the very old Natives remembered a time when there were elephants there, and I was sorry that the whole Ngong Mountain was not enclosed in the Game Reserve. Only a small part of it was Game Reserve, and the beacon on the southern peak marked the boundary of it. When the colony prospers and Nairobi, the capital, grows into a big city, the Ngong Hills might have made a matchless game park for it. But during my last years in Africa many young Nairobi shop-people ran out into the hills on Sundays, on their motor-cycles, and shot at anything they saw, and I believe that the big game will have wandered away from the hills, through the thorn-thickets and the stony ground farther south.

Up on the very ridge of the hills and on the four peaks themselves it was easy to walk; the grass was short as on a lawn, with the grey stone in places breaking through the sward. Along the ridge, up and down the peaks, like a gentle switchback, there ran a narrow game-path. One morning, at the time that I was camped in the hills, I came up here and walked along the path, and I found on it fresh tracks and dung of a herd of eland. The big peaceful animals must have been up on the ridge at sunrise, walking in a long row, and you cannot imagine that they had come for any other reason than just to look, deep down on both sides, at the land below.

We grew coffee on my farm. The land was in itself a little too high for coffee, and it was hard work to keep it going; we were never rich on the farm. But a coffee-plantation is a thing that gets hold of you and does not let you go, and there is always something to do on it: you are generally just a little behind with your work.

In the wildness and irregularity of the country, a

piece of land laid out and planted according to rule looked very well. Later on, when I flew in Africa, and became familiar with the appearance of my farm from the air, I was filled with admiration for my coffee-plantation, that lay quite bright green in the grey-green land, and I realized how keenly the human mind yearns for geometrical figures. All the country round Nairobi, particularly to the north of the town, is laid out in a similar way, and here live a people who are constantly thinking and talking of planting, pruning, or picking coffee, and who lie at night and meditate upon improvements to their coffee-factories.

Coffee-growing is a long job. It does not all come out as you imagine, when, yourself young and hopeful, in the streaming rain, you carry the boxes of your shining young coffee-plants from the nurseries, and, with the whole number of farm-hands in the field, watch the plants set in the regular rows of holes in the wet ground where they are to grow, and then have them thickly shaded against the sun, with branches broken from the bush, since obscurity is the privilege of young things. It is four or five years till the trees come into bearing, and in the meantime you will get drought on the land, or diseases, and the bold native weeds will grow up thick in the fields – the black-jack, which has 7 long scabrous seed-vessels that hang on to your clothes and stockings. Some of the trees have been badly planted with their tap-roots bent; they will die just as they begin to flower. You plant a little over six hundred trees to the acre, and I had six hundred acres of land with coffee; my oxen dragged the cultivators up and down the fields, between the rows of trees, many thousand miles, patiently, awaiting coming bounties.

There are times of great beauty on a coffee-farm. When the plantation flowered in the beginning of the rains, it was a radiant sight, like a cloud of chalk, in the mist and the drizzling rain, over six hundred acres of land. The coffee-blossom has a delicate slightly bitter scent, like the blackthorn blossom. When the field reddened with the ripe berries, all the women and the children, whom they call the Totos, were called out to pick the coffee off the trees, together with the men; then the wagons and carts brought it down to the factory near the river. Our machinery was never quite what it should have been, but we had planned and built the factory ourselves and thought highly of it. Once the whole factory burned down and had to be built up again. The big coffee-dryer turned and turned, rumbling the coffee in its iron belly with a sound like pebbles that are washed about on the seashore. Sometimes the coffee would be dry, and ready to take out of the dryer, in the middle of the night. That was a picturesque moment, with many hurricane lamps in the huge dark room of the factory, that was hung everywhere with cobwebs and coffee-husks, and with eager glowing dark faces, in the light of the lamps, round the dryer; the factory, you felt, hung in the great African night like a bright jewel in an Ethiop's ear. Later on the coffee was hulled, graded, and sorted by hand, and packed in sacks sewn up with a saddler's needle.

Then, in the end, in the early morning, while it was still dark and I was lying in bed, I heard the wagons, loaded high up with coffee-sacks, twelve to a ton, with sixteen oxen to each wagon, starting on their way into Nairobi railway station up the long factory hill, with much shouting and rattling, the drivers running beside the wagons. I was pleased to think that this was the only hill up, on their way, for the farm was a thousand feet higher than the town of Nairobi. In the evening I walked out to meet the procession that came back, the tired oxen hanging their heads in front of the empty wagons, with a tired little Toto leading them, and the weary drivers trailing their whips in the dust of the road. Now we had done what we could do. The coffee would be on the sea in a day or two, and we could only hope for good luck at the big auction-sales in London.

I had six thousand acres of land, and had thus got much spare land besides the coffee-plantation. Part of the farm was native forest, and about one thousand acres were squatters' land, what they called their *shambas*. The squatters are Natives, who with their families hold a few acres on a white man's farm, and in return have to work for him a certain number of days in the year. My squatters, I think, saw the relationship in a different light, for many of them were born on the farm, and their fathers before them, and they very likely regarded me as a sort of superior squatter on their estates. The squatters' land was more intensely alive than the rest of the farm, and was changing with the seasons the year round. The maize grew up higher than your head as you walked on the narrow hard-trampled footpaths in between the tall green rustling regiments, and then again it was harvested. The beans ripened in the fields, were gathered and thrashed by the women, and the stalks and pods were collected and burned, so that in certain seasons thin columns of smoke rose here and there all over the farm. The Kikuyu also grew the sweet potatoes, that have a vine-like leaf and spread over the ground like a dense entangled mat, and many varieties of big yellow and green speckled pumpkins.

Whenever you walk amidst the Kikuyu shambas, the first thing that will catch your eye is the hind part of a little old woman raking in her soil, like a picture of an ostrich which buries her head in the sand. Each Kikuyu family had a number of small round peaked huts and store-huts; the space between the huts was a lively place, the earth hard as concrete; here the maize was ground and the goats milked, and children and chickens were running. I used to shoot spurfowl in the sweet-potato fields round the squatters' houses in the blue late afternoons, and the stock-pigeons cooed out a loud song in the high-stemmed, fringy trees, which were left over, here and there in the shambas, from the forest that had once covered all the farm.

I had moreover a couple of thousand acres of grass-land on the farm. Here the long grass ran and fled like sea-waves before the strong wind, and the little Kikuyu herdboys herded their fathers' cows. In the cold season they carried live coals in small wicker baskets with them from the huts, and sometimes caused big grass-fires, which were disastrous to the grazing on the farm. In the years of drought the zebra and the eland came down to the farm's grass-plains.

Nairobi was our town, twelve miles away, down on a flat bit of land amongst hills. Here was the Government House and the big central offices; from here the country was ruled.

It is impossible that a town will not play a part in your life; it does not even make much difference whether you have more good or bad things to say of it, it draws your mind to it, by a mental law of gravitation. The luminous haze on the sky above the town at night, which I could see from some places on my farm, set my thoughts going, and recalled the big cities of Europe.

When I first came to Africa, there were no cars in the country, and we rode in to Nairobi, or drove in a cart with six mules to it, and stabled our animals in the stables of *The Highland Transport*. During all my time, Nairobi was a medley place, with some fine new stone buildings, and whole quarters of old corrugated iron shops, offices, and bungalows, laid out with long rows of eucalyptus trees along the bare dusty streets. The offices of the High Court, The Native Affairs Department, and the Veterinary Department were lousily housed, and I had a great respect for those government officials who could get any work at all done in the little burning hot, inky rooms in which
they were set.

All the same Nairobi was a town; here you could buy things, hear news, lunch or dine at the hotels and dance at the Club. And it was a live place, in movement like running water, and in growth like a young thing, it changed from year to year, and while you were away on a shooting safari. The new Government House was built, a stately cool house with a fine ballroom and a pretty garden, big hotels grew up, great impressive agricultural shows and fine flower shows were held, our Quasi Smart Set of the Colony from time to time enlivened the town with rows of quick melodrama. Nairobi said to you: 'Make the most of me and of time. *Wir kommen nie wieder so jung* – so undisciplined and rapacious – *zusammen*.' Generally I and Nairobi were in very good understanding, and at one time I drove ough the town and thought: There is no world without Nairobi's streets.

The quarters of the Natives and of the coloured immigrants were very extensive compared to the European town.

The Swaheli town, on the road to the Muthaiga Club, had not a good name in any way, but was a lively, dirty and gaudy place, with, at any hour, a number of things going on in it. It was built mostly out of old paraffin tins hammered flat, in various states of rust, 13 like the coral rock, the fossilized structure, from which the spirit of the advancing civilization was steadily fleeing.

The Somali town was farther away from Nairobi, on account, I think, of the Somalis' system of seclusion of their women. There were in my day a few beautiful young Somali women, of whom all the town knew the names, who went and lived in the Bazaar and led the Nairobi police a great dance; they were intelligent and bewitching people. But the honest Somali women were not seen in the town. The Somali town lay exposed to all winds and was shadeless and dusty, it must have recalled to the Somali their native deserts. Europeans, who live for a long time, even for several generations, in the same place, cannot reconcile themselves to the complete indifference to the surroundings of their homes of the nomadic races. The Somalis' houses were irregularly strewn on the bare ground, and looked as if they had been nailed together with a bushel of four-inch nails, to last for a week. It was a surprising thing, when you entered one of them, to find it inside so neat and fresh, scented with Arab incenses, with fine carpets and hangings, vessels of brass and silver, and swords with ivory hilts and noble blades. The Somali women themselves had dignified, gentle ways, and were hospitable and gay, with a laughter like silver bells. I was much at home in the Somali village through my Somali servant Farah Aden, who was with me all the time that I was in Africa, and I went to many of their feasts. A big Somali wedding is a magnificent, traditional festivity. As a guest of honour I was taken into the bridal chamber, where the walls and the bridal bed were hung with old, gently glowing weavings and embroideries, and the dark-eyed young bride herself was stiff, like a marshal's baton, with heavy silks, gold, and amber.

The Somali were cattle-dealers and traders all over the country. For the transport of their goods they kept a number of little grey donkeys in the village, and I have seen camels there as well: haughty, hardened products of the desert, beyond all earthly sufferings, like cactus, and like the Somali.

The Somali bring much trouble upon themselves by their terrible tribal quarrels. In this matter they feel and reason differently from other people. Farah belonged to the tribe of Habr Yunis, so that personally in a quarrel I sided with them. At one time there was a great real fight in the Somali town, between the two tribes of Dulba Hantis and Habr Chaolo, with rifle-shooting and fires, and ten or twelve people killed, until the Government interfered. Farah then had a young friend of his own tribe, by name of Sayid, who used to come out to see him at the farm, and who was a graceful boy, so that I was sorry when I was told by my houseboys that Sayid had gone round to visit a Habr Chaolo family in their house, when an angry member of the Dulba Hantis tribe had passed and fired two shots at haphazard through the wall of the house and broken Sayid's leg. I condoled with Farah on his friend's misfortune – 'What? Sayid?' Farah cried out with vehemence. 'That was good enough for Sayid. Why must he go and drink tea in the house of a Habr Chaolo?'

The Indians of Nairobi dominated the big native business quarter of the Bazaar, and the great Indian merchants had their little Villas just outside the town: Jevanjee, Suleiman Virjee, Allidina Visram. They all had a taste for stonework stairs, balusters, and vases, rather badly cut out of the soft stone of the country – like the structures which children build of pink ornamental bricks. They gave tea-parties in their gardens, with Indian pastry in the style of the Villas, and were clever, travelled, highly polite people. But the Indians in Africa are such grasping tradesmen that with them you would never know if you were face to face with a human individual or with the head of a firm. I had been to Suleiman Virjee's house, and when one day I saw the flag at half mast above his big compound of warehouses, I asked Farah: 'Is Suleiman Virjee dead?' 'Half dead,' said Farah. 'Do they put the flag at half mast when he is half dead?' I asked. 'Suleiman is dead,' said Farah. 'Virjee is alive.'

Before I took over the management of the farm, I had been keen on shooting and had been out on many safaris. But when I became a farmer I put away my rifles.

The Masai, the nomadic, cattle-owning nation, were neighbours of the farm and lived on the other side of the river; from time to time some of them would come to my house to complain about a lion that was taking their cows, and to ask me to go out and shoot it for them, and I did so if I could. Sometimes, on Saturday, I also walked out on the Orungi plains to shoot a zebra or two as meat for my farm labourers, with a long tail of optimistic young Kikuyu after me. I shot birds on the farm, spurfowl and guineafowl, that are very good to eat. But for many years I was not out on any shooting expedition.

Still, we often talked on the farm of the safaris that we had been on. Camping places fix themselves in your mind as if you had spent long periods of your life in them. You will remember a curve of your wagon track in the grass of the plain, like the features of a friend.

Out on the safaris, I had seen a herd of buffalo, one hundred and twenty-nine of them, come out of the morning mist under a copper sky, one by one, as if the dark and massive, iron-like animals with the mighty horizontally swung horns were not approaching, but were being created before my eyes and sent out as they were finished. I had seen a herd of elephant travelling through the dense native forest, where the sunlight is strewn down between the thick creepers in small spots and patches, pacing along as if they had an appointment at the end of the world. It was, in giant size, the border of a very old, infinitely precious Persian carpet, in the dyes of green, yellow, and black-brown. I had time after time watched the progression across the plain of the giraffe, in their queer, inimitable, vegetative gracefulness, as if it were not a herd of animals but a family of rare, long-stemmed, speckled gigantic flowers slowly advancing. I had followed two rhinos on their morning promenade, when they were sniffing and snorting in the air of the dawn – which is so cold that it hurts in the nose – and looked like two very big angular stones rollicking in the long valley and enjoying life together. I had seen the royal lion, before sunrise, below a waning moon, crossing the grey plain on his way home from the kill, drawing a dark wake in the silvery grass, his face still red up to the ears, or during the midday siesta, when he reposed contentedly in the midst of his family on the short grass and in the delicate, spring-like shade of the broad acacia trees of his park of Africa.

All these things were pleasant to think of when times were dull on the farm. And the big game was out there still, in their own country; I could go and look them up once more if I liked. Their nearness gave a shine and play to the atmosphere of the farm. Farah – although with time he came to take a vivid interest in farm affairs – and my old native safari-servants, lived in hope of other safaris.

Out in the wilds I had learned to beware of abrupt movements. The creatures with which you are dealing there are shy and watchful, they have a talent for evading you when you least expect it. No domestic animal can be as still as a wild animal. The civilized people have lost the aptitude of stillness, and must take lessons in silence from the wild before they are accepted by it. The art of moving gently, without suddenness, is the first to be studied by the hunter, and more so by the hunter with the camera. Hunters cannot have their own way, they must fall in with the wind, and the colours and smells of the landscape, and they must make the tempo of the ensemble their own. Sometimes it repeats a movement over and over again, and they must follow up with it.

When you have caught the rhythm of Africa, you find that it is the same in all her music. What I learned from the game of the country was useful to me in my dealings with the native people.

The love of woman and womanliness is a masculine characteristic, and the love of man and manliness a feminine characteristic, and there is a susceptibility to the southern countries and races that is a Nordic quality. The Normans must have fallen in love with the foreign countries, first with France and then with England. Those old milords who figure in the history and fiction of the eighteenth century, as constantly travelling in Italy, Greece, and Spain, had not a single southern trait in their nature, but were drawn and held by the fascination of things wholly different from themselves. The old German and Scandinavian painters, philosophers, and poets, when they first came to

Florence and Rome, went down on their knees to adore the South.

A queer illogical patience towards an alien world came out in these impatient people. As it is almost impossible for a woman to irritate a real man, and as to the women, a man is never quite contemptible, never altogether rejectable, as long as he remains a man, so were the hasty red-haired northern people infinitely long-suffering with the tropical countries and races. They would stand no nonsense from their own country or their own relations, but they took the drought of the African highlands, and a case of sun-stroke, the rinderpest on their cattle, and the incompetency of their native servants, with humility and resignation. Their sense of individuality itself was lost in the sense of the possibilities that lie in interaction between those who can be made one by reason of their incongruity. The people of southern Europe and the people of mixed blood have not got this quality; they blame it, or scorn it. So the men's men scorn the sighing lover, and the rational women who have no patience with their men, are in the same way indignant with Griselda.

As for me, from my first weeks in Africa, I had felt a great affection for the Natives. It was a strong feeling that embraced all ages and both sexes. The discovery of the dark races was to me a magnificent enlargement of all my world. If a person with an inborn sympathy for animals had grown up in a milieu where there were no animals, and had come into contact with animals late in life; or if a person with an instinctive taste for woods and forest had entered a forest for the first time at the age of twenty; or if someone with an ear for music had happened to hear music for the first time when he was already grown up; their cases might have been similar to mine. After I had met with the Natives, I set out the routine of my daily life to the orchestra.

My father was an officer in the Danish and French army, and as a very young lieutenant at Düppel he wrote home: 'Back in Düppel I was officer to a long column. It was hard work, but it was splendid. The love of war is a passion like another, you love soldiers as you love young womenfolk – to madness, and the one love does not exclude the other, as the girls know. But the love of women can include only one at a time, and the love for your soldiers comprehends the whole regiment, which you would like enlarged if it were possible.' It was the same thing with the Natives and me.

It was not easy to get to know the Natives. They were quick of hearing, and evanescent; if you frightened them they could withdraw into a world of their own, in a second, like the wild animals which at an abrupt movement from you are gone – simply are not there. Until you knew a Native well, it was almost impossible to get a straight answer from him. To a direct question as to how many cows he had, he had an eluding reply – 'As many as I told you yesterday.' It goes against the feelings of Europeans to be answered in such a manner, it very likely goes against the feelings of the Natives to be questioned in this way. If we pressed or pursued them, to get an explanation of their behaviour out of them, they receded as long as they possibly could, and then they used a grotesque humorous fantasy to lead us on the wrong track. Even small children in this situation had all the quality of old poker-players, who do not mind if you overvalue or undervalue their hand, so long as you do not know its real nature. When we really did break into the Natives' existence, they behaved like ants, when you poke a stick into their ant-hill; they wiped out the damage with unwearied energy, swiftly and silently – as if obliterating an unseemly action.

We could not know, and could not imagine, what the dangers were that they feared from our hands. I myself think that they were afraid of us more in the 23

manner in which you are afraid of a sudden terrific
noise, than as you are afraid of suffering and death.
And yet it was difficult to tell, for the Natives were
great at the art of mimicry. In the shambas you would
sometimes in the early morning come upon a spurfowl
which would run in front of your horse as if her wing
was broken, and she was terrified of being caught by
the dogs. But her wing was not broken, and she was
not afraid of the dogs – she could whir up before them
the moment she chose – only she had got her brood
of young chickens somewhere near by, and she was
drawing our attention away from them. Like the spurfowl, the Natives might be mimicking a fear of us
because of some other deeper dread the nature of which
we could not guess. Or in the end their behaviour to
us might be some sort of strange joke, and the shy
people were not afraid of us at all. The Natives have,
far less than the white people, the sense of risks in
life. Sometimes on a safari, or on the farm, in a moment
of extreme tension, I have met the eyes of my Native
companions, and have felt that we were at a great
distance from one another, and that they were wonder-
ing at my apprehension of our risk. It made me reflect
that perhaps they were, in life itself, within their own
24 element, such as we can never be, like fishes in deep

water which for the life of them cannot understand our fear of drowning. This assurance, this art of swimming, they had, I thought, because they had preserved a knowledge that was lost to us by our first parents; Africa, amongst the continents, will teach it to you: that God and the Devil are one, the majesty coeternal, not two uncreated but one uncreated, and the Natives neither confounded the persons nor divided the substance.

On our safaris, and on the farm, my acquaintance with the Natives developed into a settled and personal relationship. We were good friends. I reconciled myself to the fact that while I should never quite know or understand them, they knew me through and through, and were conscious of the decisions that I was going to take, before I was certain about them myself. For some time I had a small farm up at Gil-Gil, where I lived in a tent, and I travelled by the railway to and fro between Gil-Gil and Ngong. At Gil-Gil, I might make up my mind very suddenly, when it began to rain, to go back to my house. But when I came to Kikuyu, which was our station on the railway line, and from where it was ten miles to the farm, one of my people would be there with a mule for me to ride home on. When I asked them how they had known that I was coming down, they looked away, and seemed uneasy, as if frightened or bored, such as we should be if a deaf person insisted on getting an explanation of a symphony from us.

When the Natives felt safe with us from abrupt movements and sudden noises, they would speak to us a great deal more openly than one European speaks to another. They were never reliable, but in a grand manner sincere. A good name – what is called prestige – meant much in the Native world. They seemed to have made up, at some time, a joint appraisement of you, against which no one would afterwards ever go.

At times, life on the farm was very lonely, and in the stillness of the evenings when the minutes dripped from the clock, life seemed to be dripping out of you with them, just for want of white people to talk to. But all the time I felt the silent overshadowed existence of the Natives running parallel with my own, on a different plane. Echoes went from the one to the other.

The Natives were Africa in flesh and blood. The tall extinct volcano of Longonot that rises above the Rift Valley, the broad mimosa trees along the rivers, the elephant and the giraffe, were not more truly Africa than the Natives were – small figures in an immense scenery. All were different expressions of one idea,

26

variations upon the same theme. It was not a congenial upheaping of heterogeneous atoms, but a heterogeneous upheaping of congenial atoms, as in the case of the oak leaf and the acorn and the object made from oak. We ourselves, in boots, and in our constant great hurry, often jar with the landscape. The Natives are in accordance with it, and when the tall, slim, dark, and dark-eyed people travel – always one by one, so that even the great Native veins of traffic are narrow footpaths – or work the soil, or herd their cattle, or hold their big dances, or tell you a tale, it is Africa wandering, dancing, and entertaining you. In the highlands you remember the poet's words:

> Noble found I
> ever the Native,
> and insipid the Immigrant.

The colony is changing and has already changed since I lived there. When I write down as accurately as possible my experiences on the farm, with the country and with some of the inhabitants of the plains and woods, it may have a sort of historical interest.

A Native Child

Kamante was a small Kikuyu boy, the son of one of my squatters. I used to know my squatter children well, for they both worked for me on the farm, and used to be up round my house herding their goats on the lawns, in the faith that here something of interest might always occur. But Kamante must have lived on the farm for some years before I ever met him; I suppose that he had been leading a seclusive existence like a sick animal.

I came upon him for the first time one day when I was riding across the plain of the farm, and he was herding his people's goats there. He was the most pitiful object that you could set eyes on. His head was big and his body terribly small and thin, the elbows and knees stood out like knots on a stick and both his legs were covered with deep running sores from the thigh to the heel. Here on the plain he looked extraordinarily small, so that it struck you as a strange thing that so much suffering could be condensed into a single point. When I stopped and spoke to him, he did not answer, and hardly appeared to see me. In his flat, angular, harassed, and infinitely patient face, the eyes were without glance, dim like the eyes of a dead person. He looked as if he could not have more than a few weeks to live in, and you expected to see the vultures, which are never far away from death on the plain, high up in the pale burning air over his head. I told him to come round to my house the next morning, so that I could try to cure him.

I was a doctor to the people on the farm most mornings from nine to ten, and like all great quacks I had a large circle of patients, and generally between two and a dozen sick people up by my house then.

The Kikuyu are adjusted for the unforeseen and accustomed to the unexpected. Here they differ from the white men, of whom the majority strive to insure themselves against the unknown and the assaults of fate. The Negro is on friendly terms with destiny, having been in her hands all his time; she is to him, in a way, his home, the familiar darkness of the hut, deep mould for his roots. He faces any change in life with great calm. Amongst the qualities that he will be looking for in a master or a doctor or in God, imagination, I believe, comes high up in the list. It may be on the strength of such a taste that the Caliph Haroun al

Raschid maintains, to the hearts of Africa and Arabia, his position as an ideal ruler; with him nobody knew what to expect next, and you did not know where you had him. When the Africans speak of the personality of God they speak like the Arabian Nights or like the last chapters of the book of Job; it is the same quality, the infinite power of imagination, with which they are impressed.

To this characteristic in my people I myself owed my popularity, or my fame, as a doctor. When I first came out to Africa I travelled on the boat with a great German scientist, who was going out, for the twenty-third time, to experiment with cures for sleeping-sickness, and who had over a hundred rats and guinea-pigs on the boat with him. He told me that his difficulty with the Native patients had never been any lack of courage in them – in the face of pain or of a great operation they generally showed little fear – but it was their deep dislike of regularity, of any repeated treatment or the systematization of the whole; and this the great German doctor could not understand. But when I myself got to know the Natives, this quality in them was one of the things that I liked best. They had real courage: the unadulterated liking of danger – the true answer of creation to the announcement of their lot – the echo from the earth when heaven had spoken. I sometimes thought that what, at the bottom of their hearts, they feared from us was pedantry. In the hands of a pedant they die of grief.

My patients waited on a paved terrace outside my house. Here they squatted – the old skeletons of men with tearing coughs and running eyes, the young slim smooth brawlers with black eyes and bruised mouths, and the mothers with their feverish children, like little dry flowers, hanging upon their necks. I often had bad burns to treat, for the Kikuyu at night sleep round the fires in their huts, and the piles of burning wood or charcoal may collapse and slide down on them – when at times I had run out of my store of medicine, I found that honey was not a bad ointment for burns. The atmosphere of the terrace was animated, electric, like the atmosphere of the casinos in Europe. The low lively flow of talk would stop when I came out, but the silence was pregnant with possibilities, now the moment had come when anything might happen. They did, however, always wait for me myself to choose my first patient.

I knew very little of doctoring, just what you learn at a first-aid course. But my renown as a doctor had been spread by a few chance lucky cures, and had not been decreased by the catastrophic mistakes that I had made.

If now I had been able to guarantee my patients a recovery in each single case, who knows but that their circle might have thinned out? I should then have attained a professional prestige – here evidently was a highly efficient doctor from *Volaia* – but would they still have been sure that the Lord was with me? For of the Lord they knew from the great years of drought, from the lions on the plains at night, and the leopards near the houses when the children were alone there, and from the swarms of grasshoppers that would come on to the land, nobody knew where from, and leave not a leaf of grass where they had passed. They knew him, too, from the unbelievable hours of happiness when the swarm passed over the maize-field and did not settle, or when in spring the rains would come early and plentiful, and make all the fields and plains flower and give rich crops. So that this highly capable doctor from Volaia might be after all a sort of outsider where the real great things in life were concerned.

Kamante to my surprise turned up at my house the morning after our first meeting. He stood there, a little away from the three or four other sick people present, erect, with his half-dead face, as if after all he had some feeling of attachment to life, and had now made up his mind to try this last chance of holding on to it.

He showed himself with time to be an excellent patient. He came when he was ordered to come, without fault, and he could keep account of time when he was told to come back every third or fourth day, which is an unusual thing with the Natives. He bore the hard treatment of his sores with a stoicism that I have not known the like of. In all these respects I might have held him up as a model to the others, but I did not do so, for at the same time he caused me much uneasiness of mind.

Rarely, rarely, have I met such a wild creature, a human being who was so utterly isolated from the world, and, by a sort of firm, deadly resignation, completely closed to all surrounding life. I could make him answer when I questioned him, but he never volunteered a word and never looked at me. He had no pity whatever in him, and kept a little scornful laughter of contempt, and of knowing better, for the tears of the other sick children, when they were washed and bandaged, but he never looked at them either. He had no wish for any sort of contact with the world round him, the contacts that he had known of had been too cruel for that. His fortitude of soul in the face of pain was the fortitude of an old warrior. A thing could never be so bad as to surprise him: he was, by his career and his philosophy, prepared for the worst.

All this was in the grand manner, and recalled the declaration of faith of Prometheus: 'Pain is my element as hate is thine. Ye rend me now: I care not.' And, 'Ay, do thy worst. Thou art omnipotent.' But in a person of his size it was uncomfortable, a thing to make you lose heart. And what will God think – I thought – confronted with this attitude in a small human being?

I remember well the first time that he ever looked at me and spoke to me of his own accord. This must have been some time along in our acquaintance, for I had given up my first mode of treatment, and was trying a new thing, a hot poultice that I had looked up in my books. In my eagerness to do the thing thoroughly, I made it too hot, and as I put it on his leg and clapped the dressing on top of it Kamante spoke: 'Msabu,' he said, and gave me a great glance. The Natives use this Indian word when they address white women, but they pronounce it a little differently, and change it into an African word, with a diverging ring to it. In Kamante's mouth now it was a cry for help, but also a word of warning, such as a loyal friend might give you, to stop you in a proceeding unworthy of you. I thought of it with hope afterwards. I had ambition as a doctor, and I was sorry to have put on the poultice too hot, but I was glad all the same, for this was the first glimpse of an understanding between the wild child and myself. The stark sufferer, who expected nothing but suffering, did not expect it from me.

As far as my doctoring of him went, things did not, however, look hopeful. For a long time I kept on washing and bandaging his leg, but the disease was beyond me. From time to time he would grow a little better, and then the sores would break out in new places. In the end I made up my mind to take him to the hospital of the Scotch Mission.

This decision of mine for once was sufficiently fatal, and had in it enough possibilities, to make an impression on Kamante – he did not want to go. He was prevented by his career and his philosophy from protesting much against anything, but when I drove him to the mission, and delivered him there in the long hospital building, in surroundings entirely foreign and mysterious to him, he trembled.

I had the Church of Scotland Mission as a neighbour twelve miles to the north-west, five hundred feet higher than the farm; and the French Roman Catholic

Mission ten miles to the east, on the flatter land, and five hundred feet lower. I did not sympathize with the missions, but personally I was on friendly terms with them both, and regretted that between themselves they should live in a state of hostility.

The French Fathers were my best friends. I used to ride over with Farah, to hear Mass with them on Sunday morning, partly in order to speak French again, and partly because it was a lovely ride to the mission. For a long way the road ran through the Forest Department's old wattle plantation, and the virile, fresh pinaceous scent of the wattle trees was sweet and cheering in the mornings.

It was an extraordinary thing to see how the Church of Rome was carrying her atmosphere with her wherever she went. The Fathers had planned and built their church themselves, with the assistance of their Native congregation, and they were with reason very proud of it. There was here a fine big grey church with a bell-tower on it; it was laid out on a broad courtyard, above terraces and stairs, in the midst of their coffee-plantation, which was the oldest in the colony and very skilfully run. On the two other sides of the court were the arcaded refectory and the convent buildings, with the school and the mill down by the river, and to get into the drive up to the church you had to ride over an arched bridge. It was all built in grey stone, and as you came riding down upon it, it looked neat and impressive in the landscape, and might have been lying in a southern canton of Switzerland, or in the north of Italy.

The friendly fathers lay in wait for me at the church door, when Mass was over, to invite me to *un petit verre de vin*, across the courtyard in the roomy and cool refectory; there it was wonderful to hear how they knew of everything that was going on in the colony, even to the remotest corners of it. They would also, under the disguise of a sweet and benevolent conversation, draw from you any sort of news that you might possibly have in you, like a small lively group of brown, furry bees – for they all grew long, thick beards – hanging on to a flower for its store of honey. But while they were so interested in the life of the colony, they were all the time in their own French way exiles, patient and cheerful obeisants to some higher orders of a mysterious nature. If it had not been for the unknown authority that kept them in the place, you felt they would not be there, neither would the church of grey stone with the tall bell-tower, nor the arcades, the school, or any other part of their neat plantation and mission station. For when the word of relief had been given, all of these would leave the affairs of the colony to themselves and take a beeline back to Paris.

Farah, who had been holding the two ponies while I had been to church, and to the refectory, on the way back to the farm would notice my cheerful spirits – he was himself a pious Mohammedan and did not touch alcohol, but he took the Mass and the wine as co-ordinant rites of my religion.

The French Fathers sometimes rode on their motor-bicycles to the farm and lunched there; they quoted the fables of La Fontaine to me and gave me good advice on my coffee-plantation.

The Scotch Mission I did not know so well. There was a splendid view, from up there, over all the surrounding Kikuyu country, but all the same the mission station gave me an impression of blindness, as if it could see nothing itself. The Church of Scotland was working hard to put the Natives into European clothes, which, I thought, did them no good from any point of view. But they had a very good hospital at the mission, and at the time when I was there, it was in the charge of a philanthropic, clever head-doctor, Dr Arthur. They saved the life of many of the people from the farm.

At the Scotch Mission they kept Kamante for

three months. During that time I saw him once. I came riding past the mission on my way to the Kikuyu railway station, and the road here for a while runs along the hospital grounds. I caught sight of Kamante in the grounds; he was standing by himself at a little distance from the groups of other convalescents. By this time he was already so much better that he could run. When he saw me he came up to the fence and ran with me as long as it was following the road. He trotted along, on his side of the fence, like a foal in a paddock when you pass it on horseback, and kept his eyes on my pony, but he did not say a word. At the corner of the hospital grounds he had to stop, and when, as I rode on, I looked back, I saw him standing stock still, with his head up in the air and staring after me, in the exact manner of a foal when you ride away from it. I waved my hand to him a couple of times; the first time he did not react at all, then suddenly his arm went straight up like a pump-spear, but he did not do it more than once.

Kamante came back to my house on the morning of Easter Sunday, and handed me a letter from the hospital people who declared that he was much better and that they thought him cured for good. He must have known something of its contents, for he watched my face attentively while I was reading it, but he did not want to discuss it, he had greater things in his mind. Kamante always carried himself with much collected or restrained dignity, but this time he shone with repressed triumph as well.

All Natives have a strong sense for dramatic effects. Kamante had carefully tied old bandages round his legs all the way up to the knee, to arrange a surprise for me. It was clear that he saw the vital importance of the moment, not in his own good luck, but, unselfishly, in the pleasure that he was to give me. He probably remembered the times when he had seen me all upset by the continual failure of my cures with him, and he knew that the result of the hospital's treatment was an astounding thing. As slowly, slowly, he unwound the bandages from his knee to his heel there appeared, underneath them, a pair of whole smooth legs, only slightly marked by grey scars.

When Kamante had thoroughly, and in his calm grand manner, enjoyed my astonishment and pleasure, he again renewed the impression by stating that he was now a Christian. 'I am like you,' he said. He added that he thought that I might give him a rupee because

Christ had risen on this same day.

He went away to call on his own people. His mother was a widow, and lived a long way away on the farm. From what I heard from her later I believe that he did upon this day make a digression from his habit and unloaded his heart to her of the impressions of strange people and ways that he had received at the hospital. But after his visit to his mother's hut, he came back to my house as if he took it for granted that now he belonged there. He was then in my service from this time till the time that I left the country – for about twelve years.

Kamante when I first met him looked as if he were six years old, but he had a brother who looked about eight, and both brothers agreed that Kamante was the eldest of them, so I suppose he must have been set back in growth by his long illness; he was probably then nine years old. He grew up now, but he always made the impression of being a dwarf, or in some way deformed, although you could not put your finger on the precise spot that made him look so. His angular face was rounded with time, he walked and moved easily, and I myself did not think him bad-looking, but I may have looked upon him with something of a creator's eyes. His legs remained forever as thin as sticks. A fantastic figure he always was, half of fun and 41 half of diabolism; with a very slight alteration, he might have sat and stared down, on the top of the cathedral of Notre Dame in Paris. He had in him something bright and live; in a painting he would have made a spot of unusually intense colouring; with this he gave a stroke of picturesqueness to my household. He was never quite right in the head, or at least he was always what, in a white person, you would have called highly eccentric.

He was a thoughtful person. Perhaps the long years of suffering that he had lived through had developed in him a tendency to reflect upon things, and to draw his own conclusions from everything he saw. He was all his life, in his own way, an isolated figure. Even when he did the same things as other people he would do them in a different way.

I had an evening school for the people of the farm, with a Native schoolmaster to teach them. I got my schoolmasters from one of the missions, and in my time I have had all three – Roman Catholic, Church of England, and Church of Scotland schoolmasters. For the Native education of the country is run rigorously on religious lines; so far as I know there are no other books translated into Swaheli than the Bible and the hymnbooks. I myself, during all my time in Africa, was planning to translate Aesop's fables, for the benefit of the Natives, but I never found time to carry my plan through. Still, such as it was, my school was to me a favourite place on the farm, the centre of our spiritual life, and I spent many pleasant evening hours in the long old store-house of corrugated iron in which it was kept.

Kamante would then come with me, but he would not join the children on the school-benches, he would stand a little away from them, as if consciously closing his ears to the learning, and exulting in the simplicity of those who consented to be taken in, and to listen. But in the privacy of my kitchen, I have seen him copying from memory, very slowly and preposterously, those same letters and figures that he had observed on the blackboard in the school. I do not think that he could have come in with other people if he had wanted to; early in his life something in him had been twisted or locked, and now it was, so to say, to him the normal thing to be out of the normal. He was aware of this separateness of his, himself, with the arrogant greatness of soul of the real dwarf, who, when he finds himself at a difference with the whole world, holds the world to be crooked.

Kamante was shrewd in money matters; he spent

little, and did a number of wise deals with the other Kikuyu in goats. He married at an early age, and marriage in the Kikuyu world is an expensive undertaking. At the same time I have heard him philosophizing, soundly and originally, upon the worthlessness of money. He stood in a peculiar relation to existence on the whole; he mastered it, but he had no high opinion of it.

He had no gift whatever for admiration. He might acknowledge, and think well of the wisdom of animals, but there was, during all the time that I knew him, only one human being of whose good sense I heard him speak approvingly; it was a young Somali woman who some years later came to live on the farm. He had a little mocking laughter, of which he made use in all circumstances, but chiefly towards any self-confidence or grandiloquence in other people. All Natives have in them a strong strain of malice, a shrill delight in things going wrong, which in itself is hurting and revolting to Europeans. Kamante brought this characteristic to a rare perfection, even to a special self-irony, that made him take pleasure in his own disappointments and disasters, nearly exactly as in those of other people.

I have met with the same kind of mentality in the old Native women who have been roasted over many fires, who have mixed blood with Fate, and recognize her irony, wherever they meet it, with sympathy, as if it were that of a sister. On the farm I used to let my houseboys deal out snuff – *tombacco* the Natives say – to the old women on Sunday mornings, while I myself was still in bed. On this account I had a queer lot of customers round my house on Sundays, like a very old, rumpled, bald and bony poultry yard; and their low cackling – for the Natives will very rarely speak up loudly – made its way through the open windows of my bedroom. On one particular Sunday morning, the gentle lively flow of Kikuyu communications suddenly rose to ripples and cascades of mirth; some highly humorous incident was taking place out there, and I called in Farah to tell me about it. Farah did not like to tell me, for the matter was that he had forgotten to buy snuff, so that today the old women had come a long way, as they say themselves, *boori* – for nothing. This happening was later on a source of amusement to the old Kikuyu women. Sometimes, when I met one of them on a path in the maize field, she would stand still in front of me, poke a crooked bony finger at me, and, with her old dark face dissolving into laughter, so that all the wrinkles of it were drawn and folded together as by one single secret string being 45 pulled, she would remind me of the Sunday when she and her sisters in the snuff had walked and walked up to my house, only to find that I had forgotten to get it, and that there was not a grain there – Ha ha, msabu!

The white people often say of the Kikuyu that they know nothing of gratitude. Kamante in any case was not ungrateful, he even gave words to his feeling of an obligation. A number of times, many years after our first meeting, he went out of his way to do me a service for which I had not asked him, and when I asked him why he had done it, he said that if it had not been for me he would have been dead a long time ago. He showed his gratitude in another manner as well, in a particular kind of benevolent, helpful, or perhaps the right word is forbearing, attitude towards me. It may be that he kept in mind that he and I were of the same religion. In a world of fools, I was, I think, to him one of the greater fools. From the day when he came into my service and attached his fate to mine, I felt his watchful penetrating eyes on me, and my whole *modus vivendi* subject to a clear unbiased criticism; I believe that, from the beginning, he looked upon the trouble that I had taken to get him cured as upon a piece of hopeless eccentricity. But he showed me all the time great interest and sympathy, and he laid himself out to guide my great ignorance. On some occasions I found that he had given time and thought to the problem, and that he meant to prepare and illustrate his instructions, in order that they should be easier for me to understand.

Kamante began his life in my house as a dog-toto; later he became a medical assistant to me. There I found out what good hands he had, although you would not have thought so from the look of them, and I sent him into the kitchen to be a cook's boy, a marmiton, under my old cook Esa, who was murdered. After Esa's death he succeeded to him, and he was now my chef all the time that he was with me.

Natives have usually very little feeling for animals, but Kamante differed from type here, as in other things. He was an authoritative dog-boy, and he identified himself with the dogs, and would come and communicate to me what they wished, or missed, or generally thought of things. He kept the dogs free of fleas, which are a pest in Africa, and many times in the middle of the night, he and I, called by the howls of the dogs, have, by the light of a hurricane-lamp, picked off them, one by one, the murderous big ants, the 47

Siafu, which march alone and eat up everything on their way.

He must also have used his eyes at the time when he had been in the mission hospital – even if it had been, as was ever the case with him, without the slightest reverence or prepossession – for he was a thoughtful, inventive doctor's assistant. After he had left this office, he would at times appear from the kitchen to interfere in a case of sickness, and give me very sound advice.

But as a chef he was a different thing, and precluded classification. Nature had here taken a leap and cut away from the order of precedence of faculties and talents; the thing now became mystic and inexplicable, as ever where you are dealing with genius. In the kitchen, in the culinary world, Kamante had all the attributes of genius, even to that doom of genius – the individual's powerlessness in the face of his own powers. If Kamante had been born in Europe, and had fallen into the hands of a clever teacher, he might have become famous, and would have cut a droll figure in history. And out here in Africa he made himself a name, his attitude to his art was that of a master.

I was much interested in cookery myself, and on my first visit back to Europe, I took lessons from a French chef at a celebrated restaurant, because I thought it would be an amusing thing to be able to make good food in Africa. The chef, Monsieur Perrochet, at that time made me an offer to come in with him in his business of the restaurant, for the sake of my devotion to the art. Now when I found Kamante at hand, as a familiar spirit to cook with, this devotion again took hold of me. There was to me a great perspective in our working together. Nothing, I thought, could be more mysterious than this natural instinct in a savage for our culinary art. It made me take another view of our civilization; after all it might be in some way divine and predestined. I felt like the man who regained his faith in God because a phrenologist showed him the seat in the human brain of theological eloquence: if the existence of theological eloquence could be proved, the existence of theology itself was proved with it, and, in the end, God's existence.

Kamante, in all cooking matters, had a surprising manual adroitness. The great tricks and *tours de force* of the kitchen were child's play to his dark crooked hands; they knew on their own everything about omelettes, vol-au-vents, sauces, and mayonnaises. He had a special gift for making things light, as in the legend the infant Christ forms birds out of clay and 49 tells them to fly. He scorned all complicated tools, as if impatient of too much independence in them, and when I gave him a machine for beating eggs he set it aside to rust, and beat whites of egg with a weeding knife that I had had to weed the lawn with, and his whites of eggs towered up like light clouds. As a cook he had a penetrating, inspired eye, and would pick the fattest chicken out of a whole poultry-yard, and he gravely weighed an egg in his hand, and knew when it had been laid. He thought out schemes for improvement of my table, and by some means of communication, from a friend who was working for a doctor far away in the country, he got me seed of a really excellent sort of lettuce, such as I had myself for many years looked for in vain.

He had a great memory for recipes. He could not read and he knew no English, so that cookery books were of no use to him, but he must have held all that he was ever taught stored up in his ungraceful head, according to some systematization of his own, which I should never know. He had named the dishes after some event which had taken place on the day they had been shown to him, and he spoke of the sauce of the lightning that struck the tree, and of the sauce of the grey horse that died. But he did not confound any two of these things. There was only one point that I tried to impress upon him without any success: that was the order of the courses within a meal. It became necessary to me, when I had guests for dinner, to draw up for my chef as it were a pictorial menu: first a soup-plate, then a fish, then a partridge, or an artichoke. I did not quite believe this shortcoming in him to be due to a faulty memory, but he did, I think, in his own heart, maintain that there is a limit to everything and that upon anything so completely immaterial, he would not waste his time.

It is a moving thing to work together with a demon. Nominally the kitchen was mine, but in the course of our cooperation, I felt not only the kitchen, but the whole world in which we were cooperating, pass over into Kamante's hands. For here he understood to perfection what I wished of him, and sometimes he carried out my wishes even before I had told him of them; but as to me I could not make clear to myself how or indeed why he worked as he did. It seemed to me a strange thing that anyone could be so great in an art of which he did not understand the real meaning, and for which he felt nothing but contempt.

Kamante could have no idea as to how a dish of ours ought to taste, and he was, in spite of his conversion, and his connection with civilization, at heart an arrant Kikuyu, rooted in the traditions of his tribe and in his faith in them, as in the only way of living worthy of a human being. He did at times taste the food that he cooked, but then with a distrustful face, like a witch who takes a sip out of her cauldron. He stuck to the maize-cobs of his fathers. Here even his intelligence sometimes failed him, and he came and offered me a Kikuyu delicacy – a roasted sweet potato or a lump of sheep's fat – as even a civilized dog, that has lived for a long time with people, will place a bone on the floor before you, as a present. In his heart he did, I feel, all the time, look upon the trouble that we give ourselves about our food as upon a lunacy. I sometimes tried to extract from him his views upon these things, but although he spoke with great frankness on many subjects, on others he was very close, so that we worked side by side in the kitchen, leaving one another's ideas on the importance of cooking alone.

I sent Kamante into the Muthaiga Club to learn, and to the cooks of my friends in Nairobi, when I had had a new good dish in their house, and by the time that he had served his apprenticeship, my own house became famous in the colony for its table. This was a great pleasure to me. I longed to have an audience for my art, and I was glad when my friends came out to dine with me; but Kamante cared for the praise of no one. All the same he remembered the individual taste of those of my friends who came most often to the farm. 'I shall cook the fish in white wine for Bwana Berkeley Cole,' he said, gravely, as if he were speaking of a demented person. 'He sends you out white wine himself to cook fish in.' To get the opinion of an authority, I asked my old friend, Mr Charles Bulpett of Nairobi, out to dine with me. Mr Bulpett was a great traveller of the former generation, themselves a generation away from Phineas Fogg; he had been all over the world and had tasted everywhere the best it had to offer, and he had not cared to secure his future so long as he could enjoy the present moment. The books about sport and mountaineering, of fifty years ago, tell of his exploits as an athlete, and of his mountain climbings in Switzerland and Mexico, and there is a book of famous bets called *Light Come Light Go*, in which you can read of how for a bet he swam the Thames in evening clothes and a high hat – but later on, and more romantically, he swam the Hellespont like Leander and Lord Byron. I was happy when he came out to the farm for a *tête-à-tête* dinner; there is a particular happiness in giving a man whom you like very much good food that you have cooked yourself. In return he gave me his ideas on food, and on many other things in the world, and told me that he had nowhere dined better.

The Prince of Wales did me the great honour to come and dine at the farm, and to compliment me on a Cumberland sauce. This is the only time that I have seen Kamante listening with deep interest when I repeated the praise of his cooking to him, for Natives have very great ideas of kings and like to talk about them. Many months after, he felt a longing to hear it once more, and suddenly asked me, like a French reading-book, 'Did the son of the Sultan like the sauce of the pig? Did he eat it all?'

Kamante showed his good will towards me outside of the kitchen as well. He wanted to help me, in accordance with his own ideas of the advantages and dangers in life.

One night, after midnight, he suddenly walked into my bedroom with a hurricane-lamp in his hand, silent, as if on duty. It must have been only a short time after he first came into my house, for he was very small; he stood by my bedside like a dark bat that had strayed into the room, with very big spreading ears, or like a small African will-o'-the-wisp, with his lamp in his hand. He spoke to me very solemnly. 'Msabu,' he said, 'I think you had better get up.' I sat up in bed bewildered; I thought that if anything serious had happened, it would have been Farah who would have come to fetch me, but when I told Kamante to go away again, he did not move. 'Msabu,' he said again, 'I think that you had better get up. I think that God is coming.' When I heard this, I did get up, and asked him why he thought so. He gravely led me into the dining-room which looked west, towards the hills. From the door-windows I now saw a strange phenomenon. There was a big grass-fire going on, out in the hills, and the grass was burning all the way from the hill top to the plain; when seen from the house it was a nearly vertical line. It did indeed look as if some gigantic figure was moving and coming towards us. I stood for some time and looked at it, with Kamante watching by my side; then I began to explain the thing to him. I meant to quiet him, for I thought that he had been terribly frightened. But the explanation did not seem to make much impression on him one way or the other; he clearly took his mission to have been fulfilled when he had called me. 'Well, yes,' he said, 'it may be so. But I thought that you had better get up in case it was God coming.'

Wings

Denys Finch-Hatton had no other home in Africa than the farm. He lived in my house between his safaris, and kept his books and his gramophone there. When he came back to the farm, it gave out what was in it; it spoke – as the coffee-plantations speak, when with the first showers of the rainy season they flower, dripping wet, a cloud of chalk. When I was expecting Denys back, and heard his car coming up the drive, I heard, at the same time, the things of the farm all telling what they really were. He was happy on the farm; he came there only when he wanted to come, and it knew, in him, a quality of which the world besides was not aware, a humility. He never did but what he wanted to do, neither was guile found in his mouth.

Denys had a trait of character which to me was very precious, he liked to hear a story told. For I have always thought that I might have cut a figure at the time of the plague of Florence. Fashions have changed, and the art of listening to a narrative has been lost in

Europe. The Natives of Africa, who cannot read, have still got it; if you begin to them: 'There was a man who walked out on the plain, and there he met another man,' you have them all with you, their minds running upon the unknown track of the men on the plain. But white people, even if they feel that they ought to, cannot listen to a recital. If they do not become fidgety, and remember things that should be done at once, they fall asleep. The same people will ask you for something to read, and may then sit all through an evening absorbed in any kind of print handed them, they will even then read a speech. They have been accustomed to take in their impressions by the eye.

Denys, who lived much by the ear, preferred hearing a tale told to reading it; when he came to the farm he would ask: 'Have you got a story?' I had been making up many while he had been away. In the evenings he made himself comfortable, spreading cushions like a couch in front of the fire, and with me sitting on the floor, cross-legged like Scheherazade herself, he would listen, clear-eyed, to a long tale, from when it began until it ended. He kept better account of it than I did myself, and at the dramatic appearance of one of the characters, would stop me to say: 'That man died in the beginning of the story, but never mind.'

Denys taught me Latin, and to read the Bible, and the Greek poets. He himself knew great parts of the Old Testament by heart, and carried the Bible with him on all his journeys, which gained him the high esteem of the Mohammedans.

He also gave me my gramophone. It was a delight to my heart, it brought a new life to the farm, it became the voice of the farm – 'The soul within a glade the nightingale is'. Sometimes Denys would arrive unexpectedly at the house, while I was out in the coffee-field or the maize-field, bringing new records with him; he would set the gramophone going, and as I came riding back at sunset, the melody streaming towards me in the clear cool air of the evening would announce his presence to me, as if he had been laughing at me, as he often did. The Natives liked the gramophone, and used to stand round the house to listen to it; some of my houseboys picked out a favourite tune and asked me for it, when I was alone with them in the house. It was a curious thing that Kamante should stick, in his preference, with much devotion to the Adagio of Beethoven's Piano Concerto in C Major; the in describing it, so as to make clear to me which tune it was that he wanted.

Denys and I, however, did not agree in our tastes. For I wanted the old composers, and Denys, as if courteously making up to the age for his lack of harmony with it, was as modern as possible in his taste in all arts. He liked to hear the most advanced music. 'I would like Beethoven all right,' he said, 'if he were not vulgar.'

Denys and I, whenever we were together, had great luck with lions. Sometimes he came back from a shooting safari of two or three months, vexed that he had been unable to get a good lion for the people from Europe whom he had taken out. In the meantime the Masai had been to my house and had asked me to come out and shoot a certain lion or lioness which was killing off their cattle, and Farah and I had been out, camping in their manyatta, sitting up over a kill, or walking out in the early morning, without as much as finding the track of a lion. But when Denys and I went for a ride, the lions of the plains would be about, as in attendance, we would come upon them then and there at a meal, or see them crossing the dry riverbeds.

On a New Year's morning, before sunrise, Denys and I found ourselves on the new Narok road, driving along as fast as we could go on a rough road.

Denys, the day before, had lent a heavy rifle to a friend of his who was going south with a shooting party, and late in the night he remembered that he had neglected to explain to him a certain trick in the rifle, by which the hair-trigger might be put out of action. He was worried about it and afraid that the hunter would come to some sort of harm by his ignorance. We could then think of no better remedy than that we should start as early as possible, take the new road and try to overtake the shooting party at Narok. It was sixty miles, through some rough country; the safari was travelling by the old road and would be going slowly as it had heavy loaded lorries with it. Our only trouble was that we did not know if the new road would have been brought through all the way to Narok.

The early morning air of the African highlands is of such a tangible coldness and freshness that time after time the same fancy there comes back to you: you are not on earth but in dark deep waters, going ahead along the bottom of the sea. It is not even certain that you are moving at all: the flows of chilliness against your face may be the deep-sea currents, and your car, like some sluggish electric fish, may be sitting steadily upon the bottom of the sea, staring in front of her with the glaring eyes of her lamps, and letting the submarine life pass by her. The stars are so large because they are not real stars but reflections, shimmering upon the surface of the water. Alongside your path on the sea-bottom, live things, darker than their surroundings, keep on appearing, jumping up and sweeping into the long grass, as crabs and beach-fleas will make their way into the sand. The light gets clearer, and, about sunrise, the sea-bottom lifts itself towards the surface, a new created island. Whirls of smells drift quickly past you, fresh rank smells of the olive-bushes, the brine scent of burnt grass, a sudden quelling smell of decay.

Kanuthia, Denys's boy, who sat in the back of the box-body car, gently touched my shoulder and pointed to the right. To the side of the road, twelve or fifteen yards away from it, was a dark bulk, a manatee taking a rest on the sands, and on the top of it something was stirring in the dark water. It was, I saw later, a big dead giraffe bull, that had been shot two or three days before. You are not allowed to shoot the giraffe, and Denys and I later had to defend ourselves against the charge of having killed this one, but we could prove 61 that it had been dead some time when we came upon it, though it was never found by whom or why it had been killed. Upon the huge carcass of the giraffe a lioness had been feeding, and now raised her head and shoulder above it to watch the passing car.

Denys stopped the car, and Kanuthia lifted the rifle that he carried off his shoulder. Denys asked me in a low voice: 'Shall I shoot her?' – for he very courteously looked on the Ngong Hills as my private hunting-ground. We were going across the land of the same Masai who had been to my house to bewail the loss of their cattle; if this was the animal which had killed one after the other of their cows and calves, the time had come to put an end to her. I nodded.

He jumped from the car and slid back a few steps; at the same moment the lioness dived down behind the body of the giraffe, he ran round the giraffe to get within shot of her, and fired. I did not see her fall: when I got out and up to her she was lying dead in a big black pool.

There was no time to skin her, we must drive on if we were to cut off the safari at Narok. We gazed round and took note of the place; the smell of the dead giraffe was so strong that we could not very well pass it
unknowingly.

But when we had driven a further two miles there was no more road. The tools of the road-labourers lay here; on the other side of them was the wide stony land, just grey in the dawn, all unbroken by any touch of man. We looked at the tools and at the country, we would have to leave Denys's friend to take his chance with the rifle. Afterwards, when he came back, he told us that he had never had an opportunity to use it. So we turned back, and as we turned we got our faces to the eastern sky, reddening over the plains and the hills. We drove towards it and talked all the time of the lioness.

The giraffe came within view, and by this time we could see him clearly and distinguish – where the light fell on to his side – the darker square spots on his skin. And as we came near to him we saw that there was a lion standing on him. In approaching we were a little lower than the carcass; the lion stood straight up over it, dark, and behind him the sky was now all aflame. *Lion passant or.* A bit of his mane was lifted by the wind. I rose up in the car, so strong was the impression that he made, and Denys at that said: 'You shoot this time.' I was never keen to shoot with his rifle, which was too long and heavy for me, and gave me a bad shock; still, here the shot was a declaration of love: 63

should the rifle not then be of the biggest calibre? As I shot it seemed to me that the lion jumped straight up in the air, and came down with his legs gathered under him. I stood, panting, in the grass, aglow with the plenipotence that a shot gives you, because you take effect at a distance. I walked round the carcass of the giraffe. There it was – the fifth act of a classic tragedy. They were all dead now. The giraffe was looking terribly big, austere, with his four stiff legs and long stiff neck, his belly torn open by the lions. The lioness, lying on her back, had a great haughty snarl on her face, she was the *femme fatale* of the tragedy. The lion was lying not far from her, and how was it that he had learned nothing by her fate? His head was laid on his two front paws, his mighty mane covered him as a royal mantle; he too was resting in a big pool, and by now the morning air was so light that it showed scarlet.

Denys and Kanuthia pulled up their sleeves and while the sun rose they skinned the lions. When they took a rest we had a bottle of claret, and raisins and almonds, from the car; I had brought them with us to eat on the road, because it was New Year's Day. We sat on the short grass and ate and drank. The dead lions, close by, looked magnificent in their nakedness:

there was not a particle of superfluous fat on them, each muscle was a bold controlled curve, they needed no cloak, they were, all through, what they ought to be.

As we sat there, a shadow hastened over the grass and over my feet, and looking up I could distinguish, high in the light-blue sky, the circling of the vultures. My heart was as light as if I had been flying it, up there, on a string, as you fly a kite. I made a poem:

> The eagle's shadow runs across the plain,
> Towards the distant, nameless, air-blue mountains.
> But the shadows of the round young zebra
> Sit close between their delicate hoofs all day, where
>   they stand immovable.
> And wait for the evening, wait to stretch out, blue,
> Upon a plain, painted brick-red by the sunset,
> And to wander to the water-hole.

Denys and I had another dramatic adventure with lions. It happened, in reality, before the other, in the early days of our friendship.

One morning, during the spring rains, Mr Nichols, a South African, who was then my manager, came to my house all aflame, to tell me that in the night two lions had been to the farm and had killed two of our oxen. They had broken through the fence of the oxen's 65 fold, and they had dragged the dead oxen into the coffee-plantation; one of them they had eaten up there, but the other was lying amongst the coffee-trees. Would I now write him a letter to go and get strychnine in Nairobi? He would have it laid out in the carcass at once, for he thought that the lions would be sure to come back in the night.

I thought it over; it went against me to lay out strychnine for lions, and I told him that I could not see my way to do it. At that his excitement changed over into exasperation. The lions, he said, if they were left in peace over this crime, would come back another time. The bullocks they had killed were our best working bullocks, and we could not afford to lose any more. The stable of my ponies, he reminded me, was not far from the oxen's enclosure: had I thought of that? I explained that I did not mean to keep the lions on the farm, only I thought that they should be shot and not poisoned.

'And who is going to shoot them?' asked Nichols. 'I am no coward, but I am a married man and I have no wish to risk my life unnecessarily.' It was true that he was no coward; he was a plucky little man. 'There would be no sense in it,' he said. No, I said, I did not

mean to make him shoot the lions. But Mr Finch-

Hatton had arrived the night before and was in the house, he and I would go. 'Oh, that is OK,' said Nichols.

I then went in to find Denys. 'Come now,' I said to him, 'and let us go and risk our lives unnecessarily. For if they have got any value at all it is this, that they have got none. *Frei lebt wer sterben kann.*'

We went down and found the dead bullock in the coffee-plantation, as Nichols had told me; it had hardly been touched by the lions. Their spoor was deep and clear in the soft ground, two big lions had been here in the night. It was easy to follow through the plantation and up to the wood round Belknap's house, but by the time that we came there it had rained so heavily that it was difficult to see anything, and in the grass and the bush at the edge of the wood we lost the track.

'What do you think, Denys,' I asked him. 'Will they come back tonight?'

Denys had great experience with lions. He said that they would come back early in the night to finish the meat, and that we ought to give them time to settle down on it, and go down to the field ourselves at nine o'clock. We would have to use an electric torch from his safari outfit to shoot by, and he gave me the choice of the roles, but I would rather let him shoot and myself hold the torch for him.

In order that we might find our way up to the dead ox in the dark, we cut up strips of paper and fastened them on the rows of coffee-trees between which we meant to walk, marking our way in the manner of Hanzl and Gretl with their little white stones. It would take us straight to the kill, and at the end of it, twenty yards from the carcass, we tied a larger piece of paper to the tree, for here we would stop, sweep the light on and shoot. Late in the afternoon, when we took out the torch to try it, we found that the batteries of it had been running down and that the light it gave was only faint. There was no time to go into Nairobi with it now, so that we should have to make the best of it as it was.

It was the day before Denys's birthday, and while we dined, he was in a melancholic mood, reflecting that he had not had enough out of life till now. But something, I consoled him, might still happen to him before his birthday morning. I told Juma to get out a bottle of wine to be ready for us when we should come back. I kept on thinking of the lions; where would they be now, at this moment? Were they crossing the river, slowly, silently, the one in front of the other, the gentle cold flow of the river turning round their chests and flanks?

At nine o'clock we went out.

It rained a little, but there was a moon; from time to time she put out her dim white face high up in the sky, behind layers and layers of thin clouds, and was then dimly mirrored in the white-flowering coffee-field. We passed the school at a distance; it was all lighted up.

At this sight a great wave of triumph and of pride in my people swept through me. I thought of King Solomon, who says: 'The slothful man saith, There is a lion in the way; a lion is in the streets.' Here were two lions just outside their door, but my school-children were not slothful and had not let the lions keep them from school.

We found our marked two rows of coffee-trees, paused a moment, and proceeded up between them, one in front of the other. We had moccasins on, and walked silently. I began to shake and tremble with excitement. I dared not come too near to Denys for fear that he might feel it and send me back, but I dared not keep too far away from him either, for he might need my torchlight any moment.

The lions, we found afterwards, had been on the

kill. When they heard us, or smelt us, they had walked off it a little way into the coffee-field to let us pass. Probably because they thought that we were passing too slowly, the one of them gave a very low hoarse growl, in front and to the right of us. It was so low that we were not even sure that we had heard it. Denys stopped a second; without turning he asked me: 'Did you hear?'

'Yes,' I said.

We walked a little again and the deep growling was repeated, this time straight to the right. 'Put on the light,' Denys said. It was not altogether an easy job, for he was much taller than I, and I had to get the light over his shoulder on to his rifle and farther on. As I lighted the torch the whole world changed into a brilliantly lighted stage, the wet leaves of the coffee-trees shone, the clods of the ground showed up quite clearly.

First the circle of light struck a little wide-eyed jackal, like a small fox; I moved it on, and there was the lion. He stood facing us straight, and he looked very light, with all the black African night behind him. When the shot fell, close to me, I was unprepared for it, even without comprehension of what it meant, as if it had been thunder, as if I had been myself shifted into the place of the lion. He went down like a stone. 'Move on, move on,' Denys cried to me. I turned the torch farther on, but my hand shook so badly that the circle of light, which held all the world, and which I commanded, danced a dance. I heard Denys laugh beside me in the dark – 'The torch-work on the second lion,' he said to me later, 'was a little shaky.' But in the centre of the dance was the second lion, going away from us and half hidden by a coffee-tree. As the light reached him he turned his head and Denys shot. He fell out of the circle, but got up and into it again, he swung round towards us, and just as the second shot fell, he gave one long irascible groan.

Africa, in a second, grew endlessly big, and Denys and I, standing upon it, infinitely small. Outside our torchlight there was nothing but darkness, in the darkness in two directions there were lions, and from the sky rain. But when the deep roar died out, there was no movement anywhere, and the lion lay still, his head turned away on to his side, as in a gesture of disgust. There were two big dead animals in the coffee-field, and the silence of night all around.

We walked up to the lions and paced out the distance. From where we had stood the first lion was thirty yards away and the other twenty-five. They were 71 both full-grown, young, strong, fat lions. The two close friends, out in the hills or on the plains, yesterday had taken the same great adventure into their heads, and in it they had died together.

By now all the schoolchildren were coming out of the school, pouring down the road to stop in sight of us and there to cry out in a low soft voice: 'Msabu. Are you there? Are you there? Msabu, msabu.'

I sat on a lion and cried back to them: 'Yes, I am.'

Then they went on, louder and more boldly: 'Has Bedâr shot the lions? Both two?' When they found that it was so, they were at once all over the place, like a swarm of small spring-hares of the night, jumping up and down. They, then and there, made a song upon the event; it ran as follows: 'Three shots. Two lions. Three shots. Two lions.' They embroidered and embellished it as they sang it, one clear voice falling in after the other: 'Three good shots, two big strong bad kali lions.' And then they all joined into an intoxicated refrain: 'A. B. C. D.' – because they came straight from the school, and had their heads filled with wisdom.

In a short time a great number of people came to
the spot, the labourers from the mill, the squatters

of the near manyattas, and my houseboys, carrying hurricane-lamps. They stood round the lions and talked about them, then Kanuthia and the *sice*, who had brought knives, set to skin them. It was the skin of one of these lions that, later, I gave to the Indian High Priest. Pooran Singh himself appeared on the stage, in a négligée which made him look unbelievably slight, his meliferous Indian smile shone in the midst of his thick black beard, he stuttered with delight when he spoke. He was anxious to procure for himself the fat of the lions, that with his people is held in high esteem as a medicine – from the pantomime by which he expressed himself to me, I believe against rheumatism and impotence. With all this the coffee-field became very lively, the rain stopped, the moon shone down on them all.

We went back to the house and Juma brought and opened our bottle. We were too wet, and too dirty with mud and blood to sit down to it, but stood up before a flaming fire in the dining-room and drank our live, singing wine up quickly. We did not speak one word. In our hunt we had been a unity and we had nothing to say to one another.

Our friends got a good deal of entertainment out of our adventure. Old Mr Bulpett when next we came in to a dance at the Club would not speak to us the whole evening.

To Denys Finch-Hatton I owe what was, I think, the greatest, the most transporting pleasure of my life on the farm: I flew with him over Africa. There, where there are few or no roads and where you can land on the plains, flying becomes a thing of real and vital importance in your life, it opens up a world. Denys had brought out his Moth machine; it could land on my plain on the farm only a few minutes from the house, and we were up nearly every day.

You have tremendous views as you get up above the African highlands, surprising combinations and changes of light and colouring, the rainbow on the green sunlit land, the gigantic upright clouds and big wild black storms, all swing round you in a race and a dance. The lashing hard showers of rain whiten the air askance. The language is short of words for the experiences of flying, and will have to invent new words with time. When you have flown over the Rift Valley and the volcanoes of Suswa and Longonot, you have travelled far and have been to the lands on the other side of the moon. You may at other times fly low enough to see the animals on the plains and to feel towards them as God did when he had just created them, and before he commissioned Adam to give them names.

But it is not the visions but the activity which makes you happy, and the joy and glory of the flyer is the flight itself. It is a sad hardship and slavery to people who live in towns, that in all their movements they know of one dimension only; they walk along the line as if they were led on a string. The transition from the line to the plane into the two dimensions, when you wander across a field or through a wood, is a splendid liberation to the slaves, like the French Revolution. But in the air you are taken into the full freedom of the three dimensions; after long ages of exile and dreams the homesick heart throws itself into the arms of space. The laws of gravitation and time,

> . . . in life's green grove,
> Sport like tame beasts, none knew how
> gentle they could be!

Every time that I have gone up in an aeroplane and looking down have realized that I was free of the ground, I have had the consciousness of a great new discovery. 'I see,' I have thought. 'This was the idea. And now I understand everything.'

One day Denys and I flew to Lake Natron, ninety miles south-east of the farm, and more than four thousand feet lower, two thousand feet above sea level. Lake Natron is the place from where they take soda. The bottom of the lake and the shores are like some sort of whitish concrete, with a strong, sour and salt smell.

The sky was blue, but as we flew from the plains in over the stony and bare lower country, all colour seemed to be scorched out of it. The whole landscape below us looked like delicately marked tortoise-shell. Suddenly, in the midst of it was the lake. The white bottom, shining through the water, gives it, when seen from the air, a striking, an unbelievable azure colour so clear that for a moment you shut your eyes at it; the expanse of water lies in the bleak tawny land like a big bright aquamarine. We had been flying high, now we went down, and as we sank our own shade, dark blue, floated under us upon the light blue lake. Here live thousands of flamingos, although I do not know how they exist in the brackish water – surely there are no fish here. At our approach they spread out in large circles and fans, like the rays of a setting sun, like an artful Chinese pattern on silk or porcelain, forming itself and changing, as we looked at it.

We landed on the white shore, that was white-hot as an oven, and lunched there, taking shelter against the sun under the wing of the aeroplane. If you stretched out your hand from the shade, the sun was so hot that it hurt you. Our bottles of beer when they first arrived with us, straight out of the ether, were pleasantly cold, but before we had finished them, in a quarter of an hour, they became as hot as a cup of tea.

While we were lunching, a party of Masai warriors appeared on the horizon, and approached quickly. They must have spied the aeroplane landing from a distance, and resolved to have a close look at it, and a walk of any length, even in a country like this, means nothing to a Masai. They came along, the one in front of the other, naked, tall and narrow, their weapons glinting; dark like peat on the yellow-grey sand. At the feet of each of them lay and marched a small pool of shadow: these were, besides our own, the only shadows in the country as far as the eye reached. When they came up to us they fell in line, there were five of them. They stuck their heads together and began to talk to one another about the aeroplane and us. A generation ago they would have been fatal to us to meet. After a time one of them advanced and spoke to us. As they could only speak Masai and we understood but little of the language, the conversation soon slackened, he stepped back to his fellows and a few minutes later they all turned their backs upon us, and walked away, in single file, with the wide white burning salt-plain before them.

'Would you care,' said Denys, 'to fly to Naivasha? But the country lying between is very rough, we could not possibly land anywhere on the way. So we shall have to go up high and keep up at twelve thousand feet.'

The flight from Lake Natron to Naivasha was *das Ding an sich*. We took a beeline, and kept at twelve thousand feet all the way, which is so high that there is nothing to look down for. At Lake Natron I had taken off my lambskin-lined cap, now up here the air squeezed my forehead, as cold as iced water; all my hair flew backwards as if my head was being pulled off. This path, in fact, was the same as was, in the opposite direction, every evening taken by the Roc, when, with an elephant for her young in each talon, she swished from Uganda home to Arabia. Where you are sitting in front of your pilot, with nothing but space before you, you feel that he is carrying you upon the outstretched palms of his hands, as the Djinn carried Prince Ali through the air, and that the wings that bear you onward are his. We landed at the farm of our friends at Naivasha; the mad diminutive houses, and the very small trees surrounding them, all threw themselves flat upon their backs as they saw us descending.

When Denys and I had not time for long journeys we went out for a short flight over the Ngong Hills, generally about sunset. These hills, which are amongst the most beautiful in the world, are perhaps at their loveliest seen from the air, when the ridges, bare towards the four peaks, mount, and run side by side with the aeroplane, or suddenly sink down and flatten out into a small lawn.

Here in the hills were buffaloes. I had even, in my very young days – when I could not live till I had killed a specimen of each kind of African game – shot a bull out here. Later on, when I was not so keen to shoot as to watch the wild animals, I had been out to see them again. I had camped in the hills by a spring half way to the top, bringing my servants, tents, and provisions with me, and Farah and I had been up in the dark, ice-cold mornings to creep and crawl through bush and long grass, in the hope of catching a glimpse of the herd; but twice I had had to go back without success. That the herd lived there, neighbours of mine to the west, was still a value in the life on the farm, but they were serious-minded, self-sufficient neighbours, the old nobility of the hills, now somehow reduced; they did not receive much.

But one afternoon as I was having tea with some friends of mine from up-country, outside the house, Denys came flying from Nairobi and went over our heads out westwards; a little while after he turned and came back and landed on the farm. Lady Delamere and I drove down to the plain to fetch him up, but he would not get out of his aeroplane.

'The buffalo are out feeding in the hills,' he said, 'come out and have a look at them.'

'I cannot come,' I said. 'I have got a tea-party up at the house.'

'But we will go and see them and be back in a quarter of an hour,' said he.

This sounded to me like the propositions which people make to you in a dream. Lady Delamere would not fly, so I went up with him. We flew in the sun, but the hillside lay in a transparent brown shade, which soon we got into. It did not take us long to spy the buffalo from the air. Upon one of the long rounded green ridges which run, like folds of a cloth gathered together at each peak, down the side of the Ngong mountain, a herd of twenty-seven buffalo were grazing. First we saw them a long way below us, like mice moving gently on a floor, but we dived down, circling over and along their ridge, a hundred and fifty feet above them and well within shooting distance; we counted them as they peacefully blended and separated. There was one very old big black bull in the herd, one or two younger bulls, and a number of calves. The open stretch of sward upon which they walked was closed in by bush; had a stranger approached on the ground they would have heard or scented him at once, but they were not prepared for advance from the air. We had to keep moving above them all the time. They heard the noise of our machine and stopped grazing, but they did not seem to have it in them to look up. In the end they realized that something very strange was about; the old bull first walked out in front of the herd, raising his hundredweight horns, braving the unseen enemy, his four feet planted on the ground – suddenly he began to trot down the ridge and after a moment he broke into a canter. The whole clan now followed him, stampeding headlong down, and as they switched and plunged into the bush, dust and loose stones rose in their wake. In the thicket they stopped and kept close together: it looked as if a small glade in the hill had been paved with dark grey stones. Here they believed themselves to be covered to the view, and so they were to anything moving along the ground, but they could not hide themselves from the eyes of the bird of the air. We flew up and away. It was like having been taken into the heart of the Ngong Hills by a secret unknown road.

When I came back to my tea-party, the teapot on the stone table was still so hot that I burned my fingers on it. The prophet had the same experience when he upset a jug of water, and the Archangel Gabriel took him, and flew with him through the seven heavens, and when he returned, the water had not yet run out of the jug.

In the Ngong Hills there also lived a pair of eagles. Denys in the afternoons used to say: 'Let us go and visit the eagles.' I have once seen one of them sitting on a stone near the top of the mountain, and getting up from it, but otherwise they spent their life up in the air. Many times we have chased one of these eagles, careening and throwing ourselves on to one wing and then to the other, and I believe that the sharp-sighted
bird played with us. Once, when we were running side

by side, Denys stopped his engine in mid-air, and as he did so I heard the eagle screech.

The Natives liked the aeroplane, and for a time it was the fashion on the farm to portray her, so that I would find sheets of paper in the kitchen, or the kitchen wall itself covered with drawings of her, with the letters A B A K carefully copied out. But they did not really take any interest in her or in our flying.

Natives dislike speed, as we dislike noise; it is to them, at the best, hard to bear. They are also on friendly terms with time, and the plan of beguiling or killing it does not come into their heads. In fact the more time you can give them, the happier they are, and if you commission a Kikuyu to hold your horse while you make a visit, you can see by his face that he hopes you will be a long, long time about it. He does not try to pass the time then, but sits down and lives.

Neither do the Natives have much sympathy with any kind of machinery or mechanics. A group of the young generation have been carried away by the enthusiasm of the European for the motor-car, but an old Kikuyu said to me of them that they would die young, and it is likely that he was right, for renegades come of a weak line of the nation. Amongst the inventions of civilization which the Natives admire and 83 appreciate are matches, a bicycle, and a rifle; still they will drop these the moment there is any talk of a cow.

Frank Greswolde-Williams, of the Kedong Valley, took a Masai with him to England as a *sice*, and told me that a week after his arrival he rode his horses in Hyde Park as if he had been born in London. I asked this man when he came back to Africa what he found very good in England. He thought my question over with a grave face and after a long time courteously said that the white men had got very fine bridges.

I have never seen an old Native who, for things which moved by themselves without apparent interference by man or by the forces of Nature, expressed anything but distrust and a certain feeling of shame. The human mind turns away its eye from witchcraft as from something unseemly. It may be forced to take an interest in the effects of it, but it will have nothing to do with the inside working, and no one has ever tried to squeeze out of a witch the exact recipe for her brew.

Once, when Denys and I had been up, and were landing on the plain of the farm, a very old Kikuyu came up and talked to us:

'You were up very high today,' he said, 'we could not see you, only hear the aeroplane sing like a bee.'

I agreed that we had been up high.

'Did you see God?' he asked.

'No, Ndwetti,' I said, 'we did not see God.'

'Aha, then you were not up high enough,' he said, 'but now tell me: do you think that you will be able to get up high enough to see him?'

'I do not know, Ndwetti,' I said.

'And you, Bedâr,' he said, turning to Denys, 'what do you think? Will you get up high enough in your aeroplane to see God?'

'Really I do not know,' said Denys.

'Then,' said Ndwetti, 'I do not know at all why you two go on flying.'

ISABEL ALLENDE · *Voices in My Ear*
NICHOLSON BAKER · *Playing Trombone*
LINDSEY BAREHAM · *The Little Book of Big Soups*
KAREN BLIXEN · *From the Ngong Hills*
DIRK BOGARDE · *Coming of Age*
ANTHONY BURGESS · *Childhood*
ANGELA CARTER · *Lizzie Borden*
CARLOS CASTANEDA · *The Sorcerer's Ring of Power*
ELIZABETH DAVID · *Peperonata and Other Italian Dishes*
RICHARD DAWKINS · *The Pocket Watchmaker*
GERALD DURRELL · *The Pageant of Fireflies*
RICHARD ELLMANN · *The Trial of Oscar Wilde*
EPICURUS · *Letter on Happiness*
MARIANNE FAITHFULL · *Year One*
KEITH FLOYD · *Hot and Spicy Floyd*
ALEXANDER FRATER · *Where the Dawn Comes Up Like Thunder*
ESTHER FREUD · *Meeting Bilal*
JOHN KENNETH GALBRAITH · *The Culture of Contentment*
ROB GRANT AND DOUG NAYLOR · *Scenes from the Dwarf*
ROBERT GRAVES · *The Gods of Olympus*
JANE GRIGSON · *Puddings*
SOPHIE GRIGSON · *From Sophie's Table*
KATHARINE HEPBURN · *Little Me*
SUSAN HILL · *The Badness Within Him*
ALAN HOLLINGHURST · *Adventures Underground*
BARRY HUMPHRIES · *Less is More Please*
HOWARD JACOBSON · *Expulsion from Paradise*
P. D. JAMES · *The Girl Who Loved Graveyards*
STEPHEN KING · *Umney's Last Case*
LAO TZU · *Tao Te Ching*
DAVID LEAVITT · *Chips Is Here*

PENGUIN 60s

LAURIE LEE · *To War in Spain*

PATRICK LEIGH FERMOR · *Loose as the Wind*

ELMORE LEONARD · *Trouble at Rindo's Station*

DAVID LODGE · *Surprised by Summer*

BERNARD MAC LAVERTY · *The Miraculous Candidate*

SHENA MACKAY · *Cloud-Cuckoo-Land*

NORMAN MAILER · *The Dressing Room*

PETER MAYLE · *Postcards from Summer*

JAN MORRIS · *Scenes from Havian Life*

BLAKE MORRISON · *Camp Cuba*

VLADIMIR NABOKOV · *Now Remember*

REDMOND O'HANLON · *A River in Borneo*

STEVEN PINKER · *Thinking in Tongues*

CRAIG RAINE · *Private View*

CLAUDIA RODEN · *Ful Medames and Other Vegetarian Dishes*

HELGE RUBINSTEIN · *Chocolate Parfait*

SIMON SCHAMA · *The Taking of the Bastille*

WILL SELF · *The Rock of Crack As Big As the Ritz*

MARK SHAND · *Elephant Tales*

NIGEL SLATER · *30-Minute Suppers*

RICK STEIN · *Fresh from the Sea*

LYTTON STRACHEY · *Florence Nightingale*

PAUL THEROUX · *Slow Trains to Simla*

COLIN THUBRON · *Samarkand*

MARK TULLY · *Beyond Purdah*

LAURENS VAN DER POST · *Merry Christmas, Mr Lawrence*

MARGARET VISSER · *More than Meets the Eye*

GAVIN YOUNG · *Something of Samoa*

and

Thirty Obituaries from Wisden · SELECTED BY MATTHEW ENGEL